TIN TOYS

1945-1975

MICHAEL BUHLER

Photographs by Ian Hessenberg

New York  Tokyo

ISBN: 0-8256-3119-X

No part of this book may be reproduced or transmitted
in any form or by any means, electronic or mechanical,
including photocopying, without permission in writing
from the publisher: Quick Fox, A Division of Music Sales
Corporation, 33 West 60th Street, New York 10023.

Originally published in Great Britain by
Bergstrom+Boyle Books Limited
31 Fouberts Place, London W1

Design by Tamasin Cole

Printed and bound in Hong Kong by
Mandarin Publishers Limited
22a Westlands Road, Quarry Bay, Hong Kong

The author would like to thank the following people
who kindly loaned toys from their collections for this
book – Andy and Tony Cullen, Patrick Gottelier, Ian
Logan and Paul Rice.

Contents

An asterisk indicates that the whole toy is shown at the end of the book.

Front cover *: Motorcyclist. USSR, 1960's, 21cm long.
This page *: Bear. Joustra, France, 1960's, 11cm high.
Back cover *: Magic Express bus. West Germany, 1950's, 16 cm long.

Introduction

The first tin toys appeared in the United States in the middle of the nineteenth century and since then countless thousands of different designs have been manufactured, sold, played with and eventually thrown away with the other debris of childhood. The tin toy industry soon spread to Europe and in particular to Germany where it flourished in and around Nuremberg.

These early toys were hand-painted with the aid of stencils, but by the eighteen-nineties the development of offset lithography enabled complicated designs in full colour to be printed effortlessly on to thousands of sheets of tinplate which could then be cut and pressured into shape.

By the outbreak of the First World War, Germany was mass-producing toys of every kind, from huge battleships almost as large as their future owners to the thousands of small penny toys that were sold by street traders all over Europe.

Between the two world wars tin toys were made in most industrialised countries, and as before they reflected the contemporary world in miniature. The Japanese also established a toy industry, which copied the European toys of the time with skill and efficiency but contributed little of their own.

The period covered by this book starts in 1945 when at the end of the war the US Zone of Occupation included Nuremberg and its toy factories. American firms were encouraged to put money into getting the Germans back into business, to produce toys for the peacetime American market. The toys made in the late forties were a mixture of new designs and re-runs of pre-war toys with new artwork and were all marked 'US Zone Germany'. They were beautifully made; often with pressings in relief to accentuate the printed designs, as in the mountain railway (56) in which the train, viaduct and mountains are all shaped to match the background. The rich colours and careful description of the landscape could be nineteenth century in style were it not for the large saloon car crossing the bridge. The clowns and novelty toys of this period also seem far closer to the world of Struwwelpeter than they do to the Cold War and the atomic bomb. They seem immersed in northern gloom, their grotesque faces patiently waiting for a better future.

The stolid workman pushing his crate (35) and the grim faced travelling salesman (27) symbolise the determined spirit of post-war Germany. The results of their labours were reflected in German toys during the fifties which became jollier and more relaxed. This can clearly be seen in the Technofix toys of the late fifties. The graphics are brash and freely painted. The landscape is crowded with neat new houses, advertising for Shell and Coca-Cola and roads teeming with brand new cars. It is a world of booming industry, consumer goods and well-paid holidays.

There are a great number of saloon cars from this period (see 72), which show the newly affluent families of Europe taking a spin. An intriguing feature of these is the artist's convention of portraying their faces on the windscreen, their profiles on the side windows and sometimes even the backs of their heads in the rear window. These add up to an almost identikit picture of the proud drivers and their elegantly-dressed wives. The interest and charm of these toys is in part that they do reflect the character of the time so well. The engineers and the commercial artists who did the graphics had no pretensions to do more than produce a commercially successful toy; but where a scale model requires that the designer stay as close to the real-life original as possible, tin toys allowed their creators a much greater degree of freedom. The most fascinating toys are for this reason never the accurate scale models but rather those that take the essential characteristics of a car, plane or animal and by subtle emphasis and simplification convey the spirit of the original whilst having a distinct character of their own.

With names like Gunthermann, Arnold, Gama, Gescha, Technofix, Tipp, Kellerman, Distler and Schuco, the German toy industry flourished throughout the forties and fifties; exporting to the US and the rest of the world. By the end of the decade however, increased production costs, Japanese competition and the great success of diecast and plastic toys had forced many firms out of business, and others into specialised areas such as model railways.

In the UK three firms, Wells Brimtoy, Chad Valley and Mettoy made tin toys of good quality during the forties and fifties such as the refreshment vans (74, 75). Many British toys are crude and naïve by German or Japanese standards, but as the sinister clown (47) and the surrealist milkman (37) show, they do not lack character. Other European countries, particularly Spain, Portugal and France produced toys principally for their domestic markets. Both the Portuguese toys in this book are made from re-cycled sardine tins, and at various times toy manufacturers have utilised all sorts of scrap tin.

The USSR and East European countries also made toys which occasionally appeared in the West. These were often based on older German toys; the original presses were either purchased or copied. They produced their own graphics which often have a recognisable folk art style reminiscent of traditional wooden toys. The motorcycle (cover) is based on a German toy and the rocket (91) is a copy of a Japanese toy designed for the American market in the sixties. This version of the rocket is more austerely decorated than the original as befits a product of the Soviet space programme. The Chinese have also made some beautiful toys, well printed and wholly original in design but the toys they make today are crude by comparison.

And so we come to the Japanese who, having earned a reputation for skilful copying during the twenties and thirties, came into their own after the war. They, like the Germans, were helped back on their feet by the Americans, but it was not until the fifties that the new Japanese firms started to make original designs. The Japanese were chiefly interested in the American market and consequently nearly all their toys reflect American culture in one way or another. Black and white police cars, USAF jet planes and chubby, freckled faces all became familiar to small boys round the world. Many of the animals and novelty toys are based on characters from cartoons whose bright and breezy outlines, strong colours and simple shapes were easily transferred into three-dimensional tinplate (see the four birds 16, 17, 18, 19). Many of these clockwork novelty toys had ingenious mechanical actions but it was in the use of small electric motors that the Japanese really excelled.

Since these new battery powered toys could run on for far longer than any clockwork motor, it became possible to design complex cycles of action to include flashing lights and sound effects as well as movement. Many incorporated an ingenious drive system allowing them to back away from any obstacle encountered and change direction. These innovations were all put to good use in a new subject for toys that appeared in the late fifties.

The Germans had already made a few space toys (such as 89 & 90) but the launching of Russia's Sputnik and Kennedy's decision to start a space programme aimed at putting a man on the moon made space flight a reality. The Japanese toy designers took up every aspect of space from science fiction to science fact. Toys based on the rockets and satellites of the American Space Agency (108) and the magnificent space station (96) stayed close to the reality or possible future of space exploration. Others, however, such as robots took off into fantasy and appeared in every shape and size. The large battery powered models often fired missiles or rattled off bursts of gunfire (102), while small clockwork ones were content to scuttle about on wheels emitting sparks.

Flying saucers were another popular subject though apart from the delicate other-worldly features of the pilot (95) they seem to have come from planet Earth.

Japanese tin toy production reached a peak of achievement in the late sixties, but the increased labour costs in the booming Japanese economy and the popularity of diecast models which became more detailed and accurate in the sixties affected tin toys and led to the decline of both quality and quantity. At the other end of the market young children's toys were being made of plastic which was cheaper and safer than tin. Safety regulations in western countries became very strict about sharp edges, thickness of tinplate and the chemical constituents of the paint used. The shops that used to sell tin toys now sell plastic and diecast and it seems doubtful that tin toys will return to favour. Those that are still made are either very simple or largely plastic. The combination of plastic and tinplate rarely makes an attractive toy as the two materials do not blend in a visually satisfactory way.

It seems then that the best tin toys have now been made, and in this book I have set out to show that some of the most fascinating and beautiful of them have been made in the very recent past. They are just as well worth preserving as the toys from earlier years which are generally recognised as being of cultural value, and which are now eagerly sought after by collectors.

1* Somersaulting monkey. *China, 1960's, 8cm high.*

2   **3**   **4**

Six frogs. Five hop but (**5**) runs on wheels.

5. *Alco, Japan, 1970's, 7.5cm long.*

6. *BM, USSR, 1960's, 9cm long.*

2. Monkey with skipping rope. *France, 1950's, 11cm high.*

7. *Kohler, West Germany, 1960's, 6cm long.*

3. Somersaulting monkey. *HMU, India, 1950's, 8cm high.*

8. *China, 1960's, 7cm long.*

4. Monkey who swings hand over hand along a string. *TPS, Japan, 1960's, 13cm high.*

9. *Grobraschen, East Germany, 1960's, 14.5cm long.*

10. *Yone, Japan, 1960's, 9cm long.*

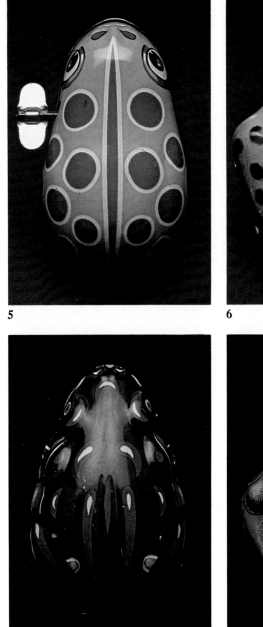

5

6

7

8

9

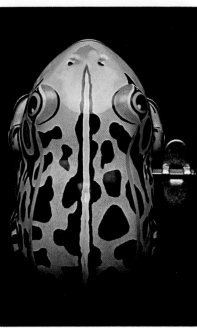

10

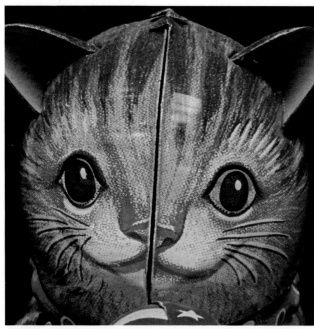

11

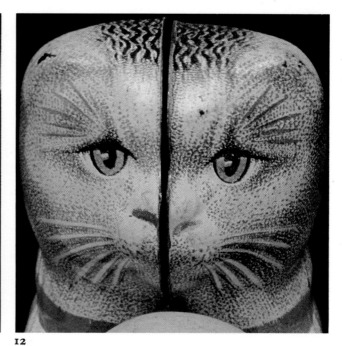

12

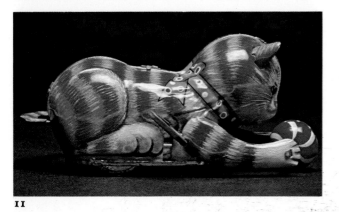

11

Cats which run round in a circle, frequently rolling over as their tails rotate, clockwork.

11. Marmalade cat. *Yone, Japan, 1960's, 14cm long.*

12. Tabby cat. *Kohler, West Germany, 1940's, 10.5cm long.*

13. Tortoiseshell cat. *MTU, Korea, 1970's, 14.5cm long.*

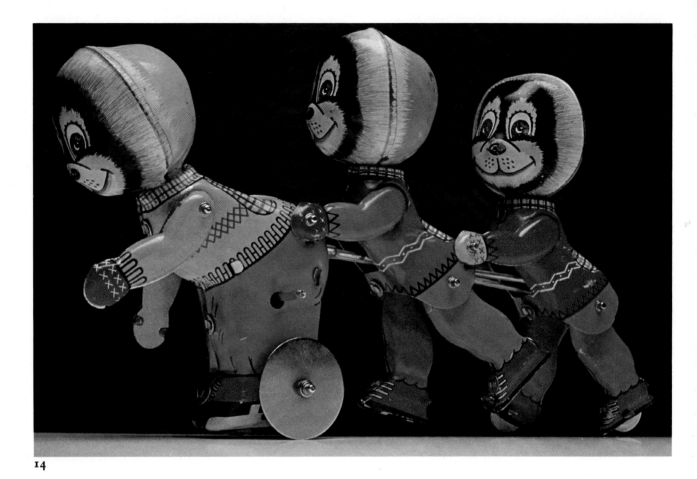

14

14. Three skating cats; move along swinging their legs in unison, clockwork. *Fino, Greece, 1950's, 23cm long.*

15. Grey dog. *Alps, Japan, 1960's, 10cm long.*

15

16*

17*

18*

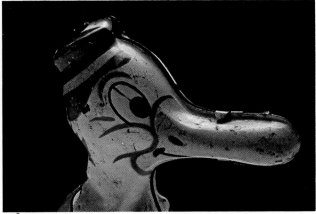

19*

16. Jim Crow. *Linemar, Japan, 1950's, 10cm high.*

17. Red bird. *Mikuni, Japan, 1960's, 10cm high.*

18. Penguin. *Japan, 1950's, 12cm high.*

19. Duck. *Chien, USA, 1950's, 10cm high.*

20. Peacock; opens and closes his tail while walking slowly forwards, clockwork. *Alps, Japan, 1950's, 17cm long.*

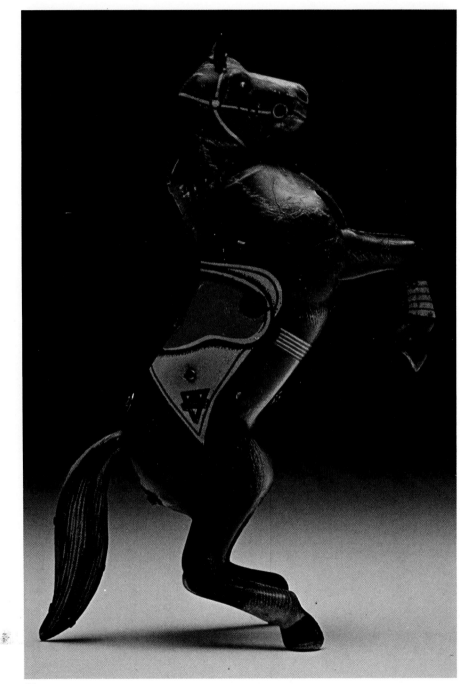

22

21. Prancing horse. *Arnold, West Germany, 1940's, 14cm high.*

22. Mother and baby squirrel. Mother and baby are joined by a string. The motor is wound by pulling the baby away from its mother. As the mother runs along the baby catches up again. *Japan, 1950's, 17cm long.*

23. Pig. *UK, 1940's, 11cm long.*

23

24*

25

26*

24. Boxers. They spar but never manage a knock-out, clockwork. *Biller, West Germany, 1950's, 9cm wide.*

25. Skier; moves forward by revolving his arms and ski sticks. *B&S, West Germany, 1950's, 11.5cm high.*

26. Fisherman. The fishing line winds and unwinds on the frame as he spins round. *West Germany, 1950's, 14cm long.*

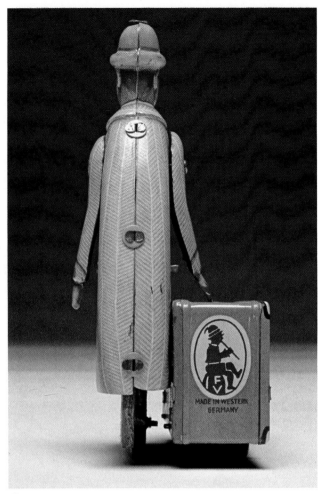

27

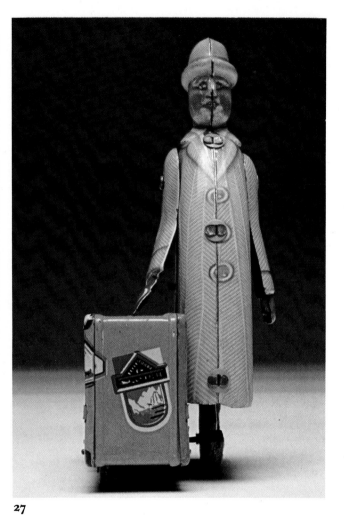

27

27. Man with suitcase. This sinister traveller has four rotating legs painted on a wheel to create an illusion of walking, and a clockwork motor in his suitcase. *FV, West Germany, 1950's, 11.5cm high.*

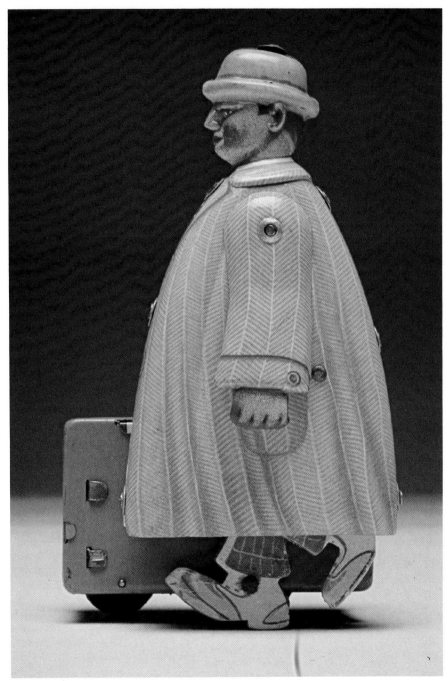

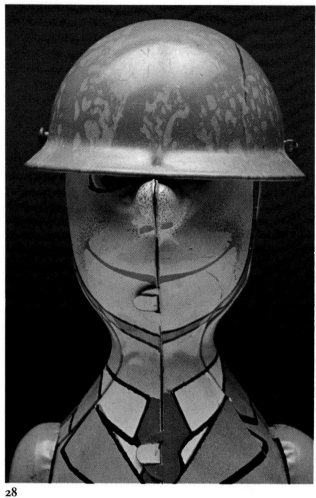

28

28

28. GI Joe and his K-9 pups. His helmet tips up and down as he walks, clockwork. *Unique Art, USA, 1950's, 23cm high.*

29. Porter and trolley. *ZMF, West Germany, 1950's, 16cm long.*

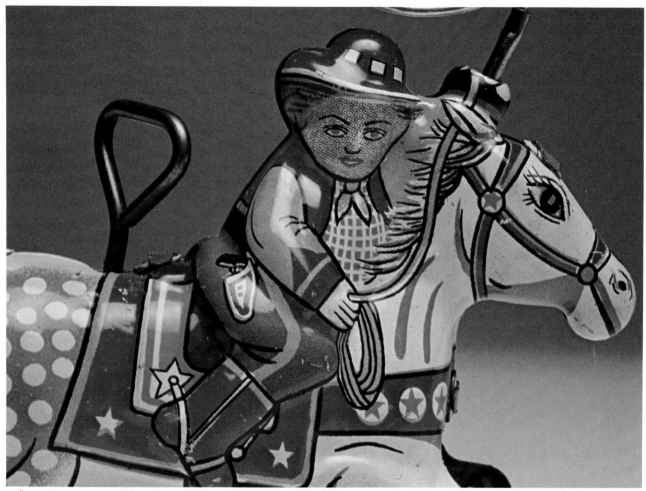

30*

Cowboys who whirl their lassoes round their heads, clockwork.

30. *Japan, 1960's, 19cm long.*

32. *West Germany, 1950's, 15cm high.*

31*

32

33

31. Red Indian. The body of the horse is jointed so that it can do a jerky stiff-legged gallop. *K, Japan, 1960's, 12cm long.*

33. Cowboy in jalopy, which lurches about while the cowboy clings desperately to the wheel. *Rico, Spain, 1960's, 16cm high.*

34

35

34

34. Policeman on tricycle, who steers a figure of eight, battery drive. *TN, Japan, 1960's, 18cm long.*

35. Man pushing a crate. The crate revolves and seems to by pushed end over end by the man who is joined to it by a wire. *WUCO, West Germany, 1950's, 12cm long.*

36*

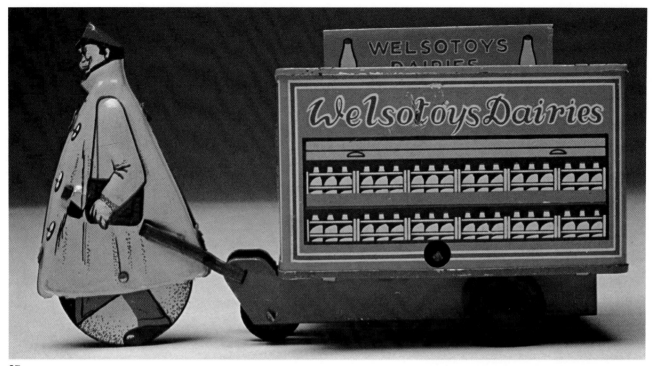

37

36. Tapdancer; executes a jerky loose-limbed dance.
S&E, Japan, 1950's, 21cm high.

37. Milk-float; the milkman walks like the man with the
suitcase (**27**). *Wells Brimtoy, UK, 1950's, 15cm long.*

37

38

38

38

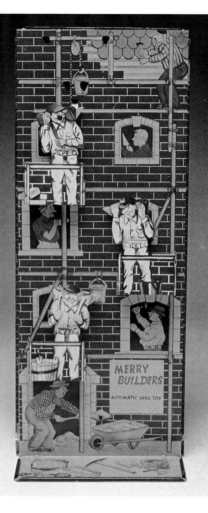

38

38. Workmen on house. Sand poured into the top man's bucket is then tipped from one to the other down the house front. *Codeg Productions, UK, 1950's, 41cm high.*

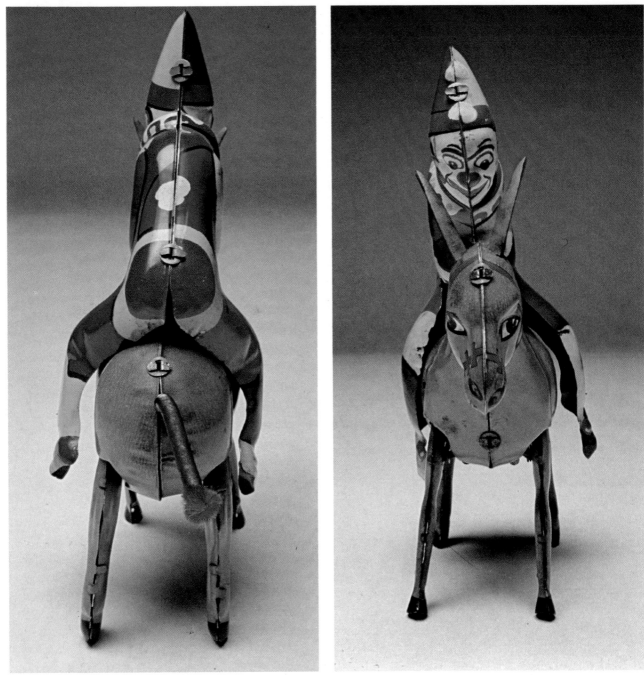

39   39

40

39. Clown on donkey. The clown almost loses his seat as the donkey bucks up and down. *West Germany, 1940's, 14cm high.*

40. Clown and cart. Apart from the artwork this is a copy of a much earlier German toy. *USSR, 1960's, 13.5cm long.*

39

41

41

41. Circus truck. *Mettoy, UK, 1950's, 24cm long*.

42. Elephant and clowns. The clockwork elephant leads a procession of spinning and somersaulting clowns. *TPS, Japan, 1960's, 30cm long*.

42

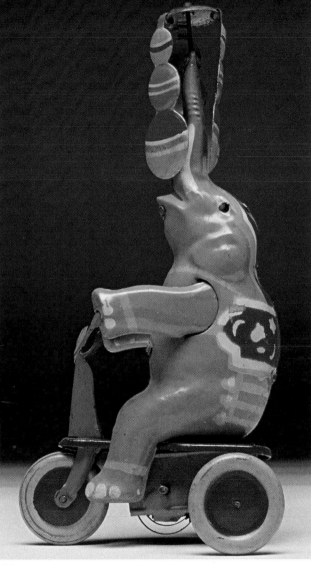

43

44

43. Handstand clown. *UK, 1950's, 12cm high.*

44. Elephant on tricycle. The propeller blades spin round as the elephant pedals in a circle. This is a crude version of an old German toy. The colours are sprayed on using stencils. *Portugal, 1960's, 21cm high.*

45. Majid family circus. The two small monkeys pedal their relatives along with enthusiasm. *India, 1960's, 15cm high.*

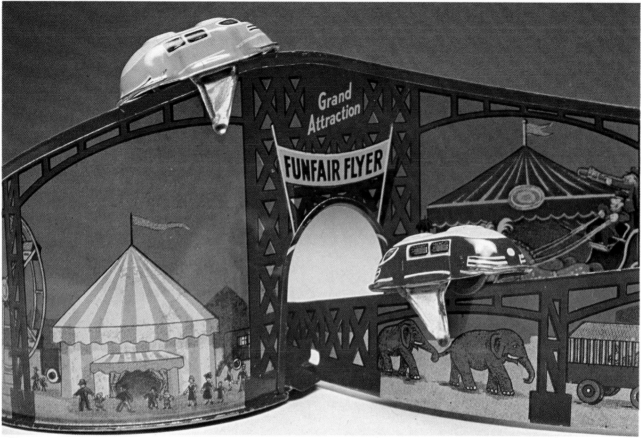

46*

46. Funfair flyer. A revolving arm pushes the cars to the top, and they then coast round and down again. *UK, 1950's, 27cm long.*

47. Propeller clown. The blades spread out when the toy is spun like a top. *UK, 1940's, 15.5cm high.*

48. Clown in car. When this friction drive car hits an obstacle the clown pops up on a spring. *W Toy, Japan, 1960's, 14cm long.*

49. Clown in bumper car. *UK, 1950's, 11cm long.*

50. Clown on motorcycle. *Japan, 1960's, 15cm long.*

47

48

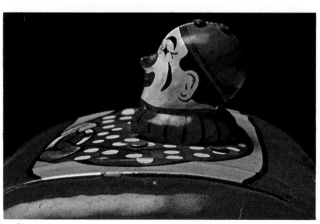

49*

50

51* Toboggan ride. The two clockwork cars climb to the top and freewheel down the track at great speed. *Technofix, West Germany, 1960's, 50cm wide.*

52

52. Clown musicians. *EHN, West Germany, 1940's, 22cm long.*

53.

53. Car and garage. The clockwork car comes out of the garage, creeps round the side and goes in through the rear entrance. *PN, West Germany, 1950's, 22cm long.*

54. Garage and three cars. *UK, 1950's, 14.5cm wide.*

55. Garage and two cars. *West Germany, 1940's, 5.5cm wide.*

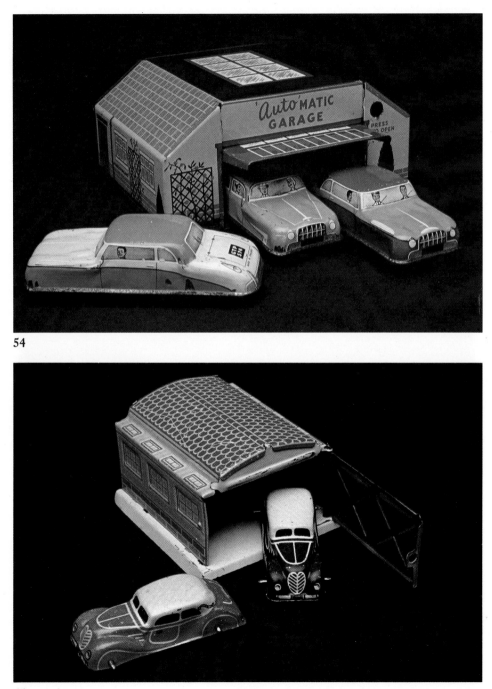

54

55

MADE IN U.S-ZONE GERMANY

56*

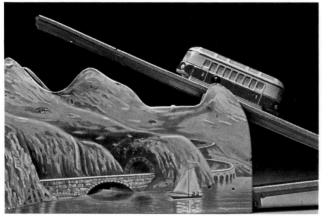

56*

57*

56. Mountain railway. *Technofix, West Germany, 1940's, 110cm long.*

57. Cable car. While the cable cars travel between the station and the restaurant at the summit, two small cars run down a road and are then pushed by a clockwork motor to the top again. *Technofix, West Germany, 1960's, 48cm long.*

57*

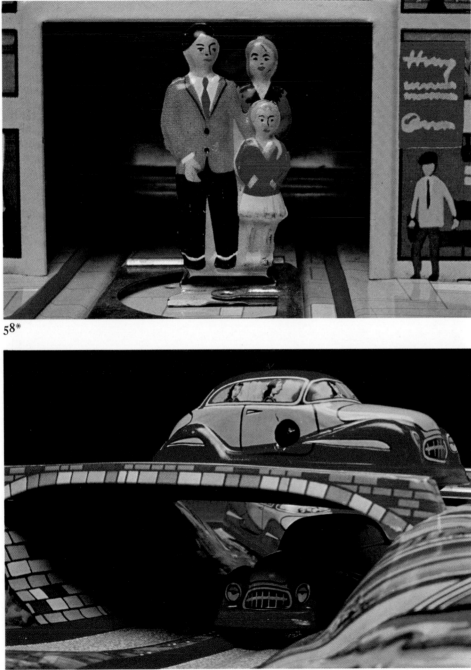

58*

59*

60*

These toys, typical of the complex Technofix products
of the 1960's, all have ingenious sets of trips to prevent
collisions.

58. Zebra crossing. The cars halt while the family crosses
the road. *Technofix, West Germany, 1960's, 33cm long.*

59. Highway viaduct. Three clockwork cars drive round
the flyover. *Technofix, West Germany, 1960's, 47cm long.*

60. Alpine railway. Two clockwork cars climb by cog
and ratchet to the top and then zigzag down via a small
station. *Technofix, West Germany, 1960's, 80cm long.*

61

62

63*

Small friction drive cars are often produced with different artwork. The most usual set (not shown here) is Police, Fire and Ambulance.

61. Three cars. *Haji, Japan, 1950's, 10cm long.*

62. Four vans. *TN, Japan, 1970's, 8cm long.*

63. Police car. *N, West Germany, 1960's, 22cm long.*

64. Bulldozer. *TN, Japan, 1950's, 24cm long.*   **65.** Tractor. *Mettoy, UK, 1950's, 13cm long.*

64

65

66

67

67

68

69

London buses and San Francisco tramcars have appeared in many versions, made by various manufacturers. They presented the designer with an opportunity to show national stereotypes as passengers in the windows.

66. Trolley bus. *Wells Brimtoy, UK, 1950's, 20cm long.*

67. Routemaster bus. *UK, 1960's, 15cm long.*

68. Doubledecker bus. *Wells Brimtoy, UK, 1950's, 20cm long.*

69. San Francisco tramcar. *Japan, 1960's, 15cm long.*

70*

71

70. Police motorbike. *ST, Japan, 1970's, 21cm long.*

71. Fire department jeep. Like the bulldozer (**64**), one of the first battery operated toys able to back off from obstacles and continue moving. Periodic halts are made for the fireman to call HQ on the radiophone. The firemen's heads are particularly well modelled with almost invisible joins in their helmet straps. Usually heads are made of two profiles (**35**, **64**). *TN, Japan, 1950's, 28cm long.*

71

72

72

72

73*

These two cars are typical of many that reflect the
higher standard of living of the 1950's.

72. Family saloon. *West Germany, 1950's, 33cm long.*

73. Convertible. *Huki, West Germany, 1950's, 23cm long.*

74*

74. Refreshment truck. Identical body to the circus truck. **(41)**. *Mettoy, UK, 1950's, 24cm long.*

On both of these vans the serving counters fold up.

75. Mac's snacks van. *Chad Valley, UK, 1950's, 13.5 cm long.*

76. Ice cream van. *Wells Brimtoy, UK, 1950's, 8.5cm long.*

75

76

77

78

79

80

77. Police cycle with side car and a working siren, clockwork. *Marx, USA, 1940's, 21cm long.*

78. Four soldiers in a jeep. *Marx, USA, 1940's, 14cm long.*

79. Motorcyclist. *Portugal, 1940's, 13.5cm long.*

80. Motor scooter. *Technofix, West Germany, 1950's, 16.5cm long.*

81

81. Group of aircraft. All friction drive. *Various manufacturers, Japan, 1960's and 1970's, average length 10cm.*

82. Thunderbolt. Friction drive. *Paya, Spain, 1960's, 20cm long.*

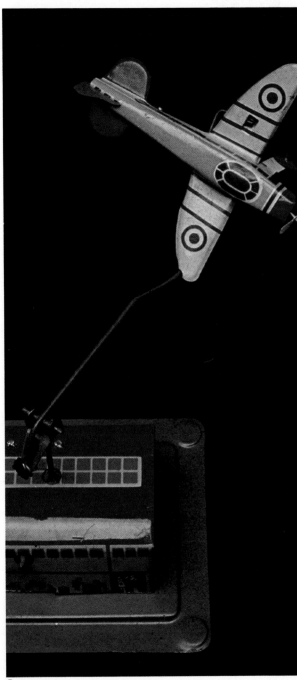

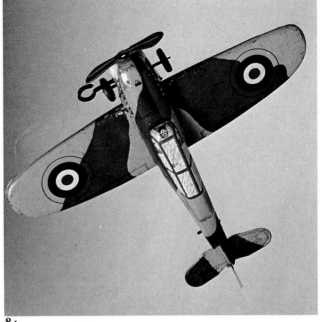

84

83. Plane and hangar. The idea of a plane circling an airport has been taken up by many manufacturers. *UK, 1950's, 30cm high.*

84. Spitfire. *Mettoy, UK, 1940's, 25cm wide.*
Three somersaulting planes. These clockwork planes all have an arm under the fuselage which periodically tips them head over heels as they go along.

85. *Yone, Japan, 1960's, 10.5cm wide.*

86. *China, 1960's, 10.5cm wide.*

87. *Huki, West Germany, 1940's, 13cm wide.*

88. Jet airliner. *West Germany, 1950's, 21cm long.*

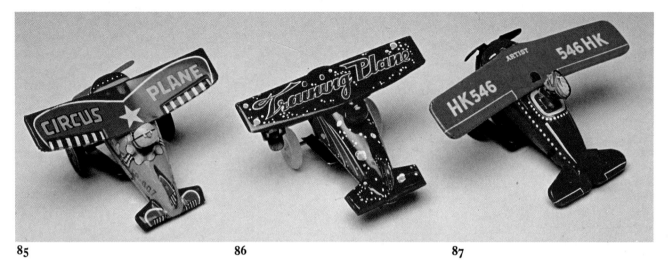

85   86   87

88

89.

89. Spaceport. The world revolves and the two spaceships rocket round the perimeter track. *Technofix, West Germany, 1950's, 37cm long.*

90. Rocket on wire. The rocket zooms up a wire fixed to the wall and then releases a parachutist who slides down the wire to the floor. This is clearly inspired by pre-war ideas of spacecraft rather than the contemporary American rockets based on the V2. *Gunthermann, West Germany, 1940's, 17cm long.*

91. Rocket. When the nose hits an obstacle the rocket stands up on its fins, friction drive. *Flim, Hungary, 1960's, 40cm high.*

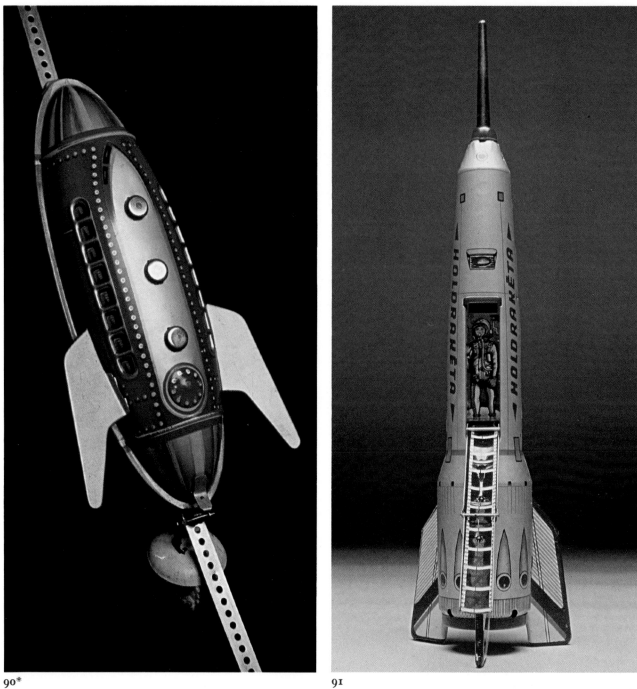

90*   91

92

93

94

95*

Flying saucers.

92. Friction drive. *Ne Kur, Turkey, 1960's, 17cm wide.*

93. Clockwork. *K, Japan, 1960's, 13cm wide.*

94. Friction drive. *Mar Ubishi, Japan, 1960's, 17cm wide.*

95. Flying saucer pilot from a battery driven saucer, with flashing lights and a penetrating 'space noise'. *KO, Japan, 1960's, 28cm wide.*

96. Space station. The space station is battery driven and moves round the floor with rotating and illuminated cabins. *SH, Japan, 1960's, 28cm wide.*

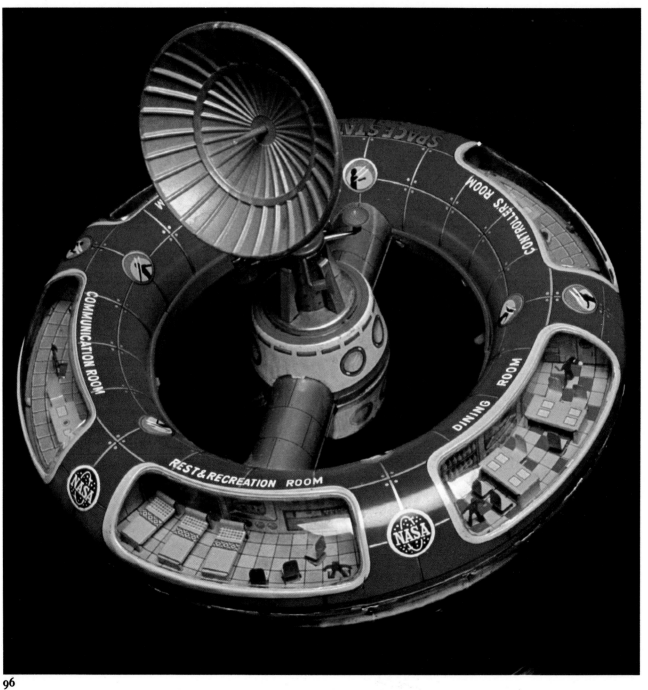

97   98   99   100

Family of robots, clockwork.

97. *Japan, 1970's, 10cm high.*

98. *N, Japan, 1970's, 13cm high.*

99. *SY, Japan, 1960's, 17cm high.*

100. *SY, Japan, 1960's, 19cm high.*

101. Spaceman. *N, Japan, 1960's, 13cm high.*

102. Spaceman. Bares his chest to fire his guns, and rotates his torso, battery drive. *SH, Japan, 1960's, 30cm high.*

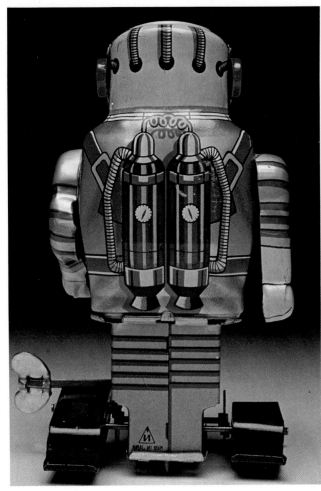

101

102

103

104

105

106

Space guns. These are all friction-drive and make sparks.

103. *Daiya, Japan, 1960's, 19cm long.*

104. *Shudo, Japan, 1970's, 14cm long.*

105. *Shudo, Japan, 1960's, 10cm long.*

106. Super Jet. Battery driven, the pilot swivels his flashing ray gun as it travels round the floor. *TN, Japan, 1960's, 31cm long.*

107*

108

109*

110*

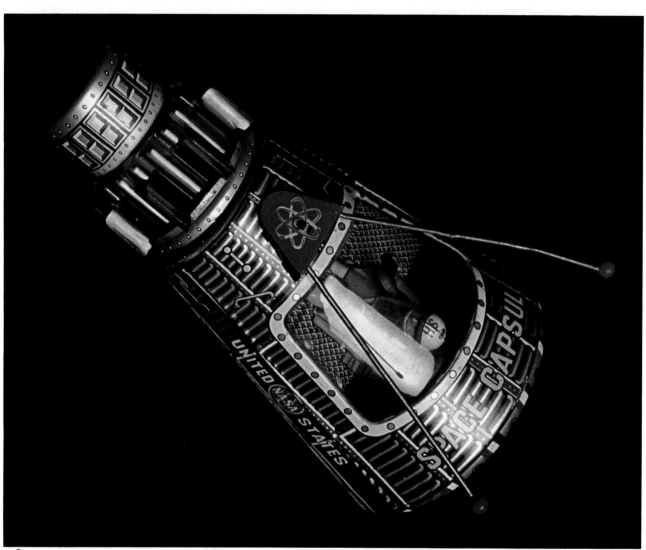

Friction drive tanks.

107. Spacetank driver. *KO, Japan, 1960's, 15cm long.*

109. Mars Patrol. The cabin dome rotates round the pilot as it moves. *MY, Japan, 1960's, 15cm long.*

110. Spacetank. *TT, Japan, 1960's, 12cm long.*

108. Space capsule. A battery driven model of an American manned satellite. A few drops of oil put on the rear end produces an ominous plume of blue smoke from its heatshield. Detail of pilot opposite. *SH, Japan, 1960's, 27cm long.*

Front cover

Contents

1

16

17

18

19

24

26

30

31

36

46

49

51

53

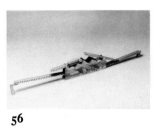

56

57

58

59

60

63

70

73

74

89

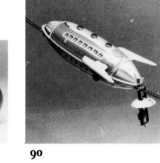

90

95

107

109

110

Back cover

Index